Painting on Stones

Geneviève Ploquin

SEARCH PRESS

First published in Great Britain 1998 by
Search Press Limited
Wellwood, North Farm Road, Tunbridge Wells, Kent TN2 3DR

Reprinted 1999, 2002, 2005

English translation by G de la Bédoyère
English translation © Search Press Limited 1998

Originally published in France 1995 by
Éditions Didier CARPENTIER under the original title: *Galets Peints*
Copyright © Éditions Didier CARPENTIER 1995

ISBN 0 85532 864 9

Printed in Malaysia by Times Offset (M) Sdn Bhd

Contents

Introduction

Nature, with its infinite variety of subjects, shapes and colours, has always been a source of inspiration for artists. Stone pebbles are just one of Nature's gifts that provide us with an ideal medium for creative art.

Pebbles can be found in many sizes, shapes and colours, and with a variety of surface textures and patterns. Look at a selection and see how their forms suggest animals, people and other inanimate objects. Add some decoration and these basic shapes can be brought to life. Some pebbles will look wonderful with a simple design painted on the natural stone colour, whilst others will be enhanced with a coat or two of gloss varnish.

The most common places to find pebbles are beaches, streams and rivers, especially fast-moving rivers with rapids and waterfalls. However, pebbles are thousands of years old and the water that created them could well have disappeared completely, so you can come across them almost anywhere.

Most pebbles, especially those collected from a beach, will have a surface layer of salt or grime which could affect any surface decoration you wish to apply. Wash pebbles with soapy water and a stiff brush, rinse them thoroughly and leave to dry. Clean oiled pebbles with a suitable solvent before washing.

Simple techniques

Transferring a design

1. Adjust the size of your design so that it will fit on your chosen pebble.

Fig.1

2. Copy the design on to tracing paper (Fig.1).

Fig.2

3. Turn the tracing over and go back over the reverse of the design using a soft, black pencil for light-toned pebbles or a white pencil for dark ones (Fig.2).

Fig.3

4. Cut the tracing paper close to the edges of the design and then secure it to the pebble, right side uppermost, with sticky tape (Fig.3).

5. Use a dried-out ball-point pen to draw over the pencilled design – press quite firmly and keep to the lines. Lift a corner of the tracing paper to check that the transferred image is visible.

Painting pebbles

Use acrylic or gouache paints to decorate your pebbles. Use a thin, supple watercolour brush to paint large areas of the design and a very small, fine brush for precise details.

Acrylic paints are good for brightly-coloured designs. The painted surface has a satin finish that can be left as it is or coated with one or two coats of varnish.

Gouache paints are more versatile but they have a matt finish and so should be covered with varnish if you want to fix the design. Increase the opacity of a colour by adding a little white paint. Dilute the colour with water and use gouache like watercolour paints on extremely smooth pebbles – the cat on page 18 is decorated in this way.

Ox gall, available from art suppliers, can be added to gouache to help it 'take' on pebbles. In fact, ox gall is good as a sole-dilutant for gouache, especially when the gouache image is to be overpainted.

Some designs require an even-width outline; use a technical pen for these applications.

Varnishing

If you want to have a gloss finish, wait until the painted image is quite dry and then apply varnish. You can varnish just the painted image or the whole pebble. You can use colourless nail varnish or gouache varnish. Apply two coats of varnish, leaving the first to dry completely before applying the next.

Varnish should enhance the natural colour of a pebble, normally making it rather darker than it was before. Test your chosen varnish on a small portion of the underside of a pebble to see its effect.

Joining pebbles

Sometimes you will want to join two or more pebbles together, either to allow your decorated pebble to stand on end or to create a jointed design. The rounded shape of most pebbles means that the contact points on mating surfaces are very tiny, so a strong adhesive bond is required. Best results are obtained with two-part adhesives – there are lots of different types, so follow the manufacturer's instructions when mixing and applying them. Pebbles can be very slippery and, although these adhesives do dry rapidly, you must hold the pebbles firmly in place until the adhesive has thoroughly set. Blobs of plastic adhesive or plasticine, or lengths of sticky tape will prove helpful.

You can also use a small piece of air-drying clay to join pebbles together. The clay will stick to the surface of dampened pebbles.

General-purpose, impact adhesives can be used to stick small, lightweight pebbles on to larger ones.

Stone faces

Gold mask

Two contrasting elements such as natural stone and gold paint, often create an interesting effect.

Aztec pebble

A big pebble and white, yellow and red paints are all that is needed to make the impressive profile below.

Dragon

Simple painting skills transform a plain pebble into a colourful dragon.

African masks

Round or pear-shaped pebbles are most suitable for these two splendid African mask designs.

The brown one opposite is inspired by a Baoulé head from the Ivory Coast. Use a fine brush and keep the point steady as you paint the lines.

The mask below requires a very rounded, dark coloured pebble that will contrast with the white lines of the design. Alternatively, paint a black background on a suitably shaped pebble and then apply the white design over this.

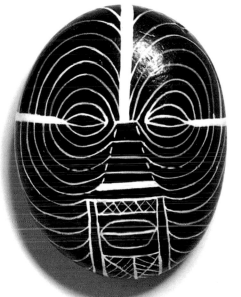

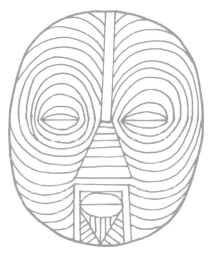

Buddha

You will have to search for pebbles of the right shape and colour for this statue. The ears and the topknot of hair are glued on to a well-rounded head. The main features are painted with diluted gouache and then a deeper wash is used to create depth.

7

Symbols

Coins

It is very easy to find pebbles that are coin-shaped. The design used on this pebble dates from the second or first century BC.

Celtic cross

This design is taken from a twelfth-century carving which decorates the gable of Caen Abbey in France. Light brown gouache is used sparingly to create the carved effect.

Egyptian cross

This very old symbol looks best on a long, slightly rounded pebble: on a smaller scale, it would make a pretty pendant.

Coats of arms

Simple designs stand out well on smooth round pebbles. This motif is painted using a very fine brush and then the pebble is given two coats of varnish.

Fleur de lys

Two contrasting colours are used to create the relief effect on this classical motif. Use light colours on a dark background and vice versa.

Shaped designs

Fan

Emphasise a design by painting it on a pebble that has a similar shape.

Window box

The background represents the walls of a house; a thin brush is used to paint on the white window frame and the bright flowers are created with dots of colour.

Silhouettes

White gouache, used like watercolour, can give spectacular results. Contrasting lights and darks bring misty silhouettes to life.

Vase

Virgin and child

Dish

Piglet money-box

Pottery pebbles

Cover a pebble with several coats of white paint and you will get an ideal base on which to reproduce earthenware effects. Leave the base coats to dry completely before adding the decoration.

The statuette of the Virgin Mary was made from three pebbles: two small ones (for the crown and baby Jesus) were glued on to a long, rounded pebble that forms the figure of Mary. The piece was decorated with shades of blue, yellow, red and black.

The vase was made from an oval pebble to which coils of air-hardened clay were added for the rim and base. It was decorated with traditional motifs.

A flat, rounded pebble was used for the delicately ornamented dish.

The piglet money-box is an egg-shaped pebble on which ears and a nose have been glued. A thin flat pebble forms the base.

Lucky charms

Symbols, signs and charms have been used throughout the ages in astrology, to foretell the future, or to bring good luck. Some of the designs on this page may be familiar to you: the Valentine heart, the horseshoe, the number 13 and a four-leaf clover. Less well-known is the red hand of Nepal, which holds in its closed palm the secret of power.

Valentine heart

Number 13

Horseshoe

Playing card

Lined palm

Red hand of Nepal

Four-leaf clover

Small scenes

Small pebbles are easily found on beaches, country roads or gravel paths. If you study their shapes closely, you will soon be able to see little figures which will suggest delightful scenes such as the ones shown here.

Red Indian

You may have to search for the triangular pebbles needed for the tepee and the Red Indian's body. The cardboard headdress is added after the scene has been assembled and painted.

Eskimos

Choose the shape and colour of the pebble for the igloo carefully and mount it on a base of white clay.

Nativity

The form and colour of the pebbles are particularly important for this subject. The cave opening is painted on to a plain, roughly textured pebble.

The princess and the tower

A long pebble is used for the tower which is topped with a conical card roof (fig. 1). The tower and the pebbles at the base are assembled with air-drying clay. The princess's crown is made out of thin painted card.

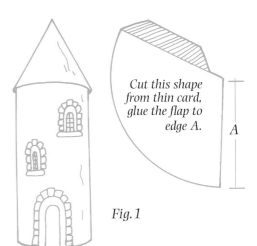

Cut this shape from thin card, glue the flap to edge A.

A

Fig. 1

The opera

Air-drying clay is used to make the singers' heads. These are painted when the clay is dry; they are then attached to the pebble bodies.

The farmhouse kitchen

Decorate the background pebble, but only varnish the fireplace. Roll out a piece of air-drying clay for the base and when it is really hard, paint in the tiles. Assemble the scene and glue the pebbles together.

Animals

Canary

Paint the cage on to a suitable stone, then glue a small, round pebble to the top. One pebble is used for the canary's body, and a small flat one is used for its wing.

Hungry mouse

Two pebbles of a different size and shape, plus a fine tail of darning thread, are all you need for this design.

Grey cats

These two little rascals require triangular pebbles for their bodies, oval pebbles for their heads, and thin ones for their tails and small triangular stones for their ears. Stick the heads to the bodies with air-drying clay. If necessary, wedge the base of each body with a small pebble so that each cat stays upright.

Koala bear

Pig

Rabbit

Bear

Animal heads

With just two pebbles you will be able to make an amusing collection of animals. Use a round one for the head and a small one for the nose. The ears can be made either from carefully selected pebbles or modelled from air-drying clay.

Monkey

Dog

Tiger

Cat

Puppy

The shape of a pebble will often suggest a subject to you. This adorable puppy fits snugly on to a triangular stone.

Kitten

A smooth, elongated pebble makes an ideal bed for this sleepy kitten. Find two similar shaped pebbles to make a pair of slippers, with one kitten asleep inside, the other awake.

Cat

The shape of this pebble is perfect for this subject. The cat's ears are made with small pieces of thin card which are glued on to the pebble before painting.

Forest creatures

Here are a few creatures that are assembled from pebbles with unusual shapes. If you can find the right shaped pebbles, you can create a range of endearing animals.

Some of the joints, and the snails' horns, are made with air-drying clay. The features and details are painted on to the assembled pieces.

Rabbit

Squirrel

Snails

Toucans

These cheerful birds have brightly coloured plumage and enormous beaks. The pebbles required to make them are quite easy to find.

Beetles

Collect a number of similar shaped pebbles to make a set of brightly coloured beetles. Paint in the coloured background, add the black lines, either with a technical pen or a fine permanent felt-tip pen and paint in the finer details. Apply two coats of varnish to enhance the colours.

Creepy crawlies

Tiny pebbles can be used to create a delightful range of vibrantly coloured insects.

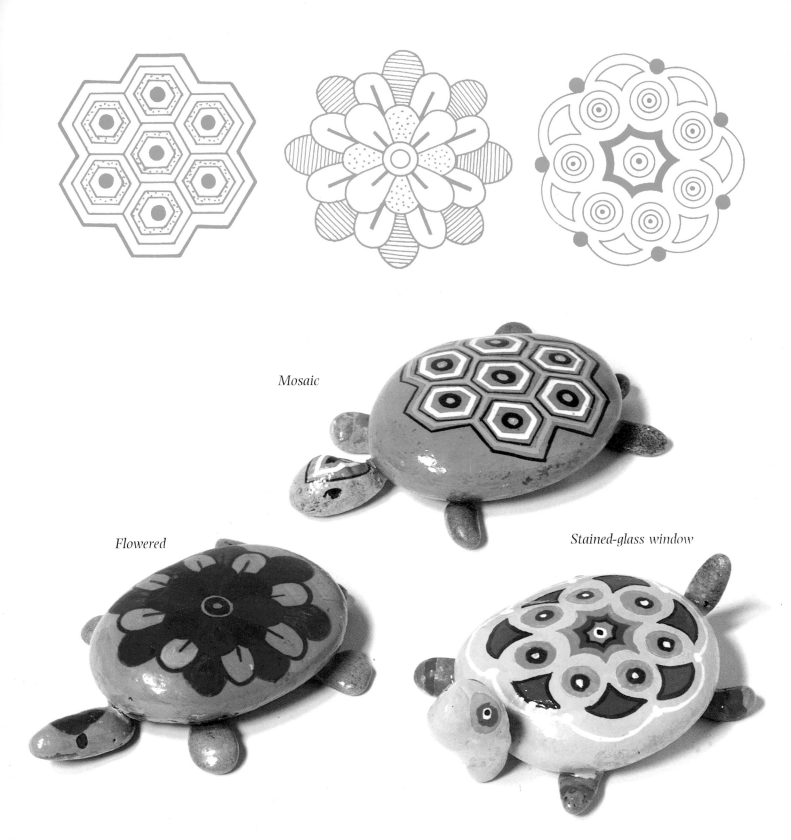

Mosaic

Flowered

Stained-glass window

Ornamental tortoises

Flat rounded stones are needed for tortoise shells.
Decorate them using designs that have radiating
patterns – mosaics, flowers and stained-glass
windows are all are well-suited for this application.
The contrast of natural stone with bright colours will
also enhance the effect. Do not forget to include a
head, which you can decorate to match the shell, the
four paws and the tail.

Sausage dog

It's fun to find pebbles which match an animal's shape exactly, and a sausage-shaped pebble forms the body of this delightful little basset hound.

Bunny rabbit

This little bunny is made from eight pebbles all of the same colour. Decoration is limited to simple details such as the eyes and nose.

Nesting duck

You may have to look very carefully to find a pebble for this duck's beak but all the others are easy to find.

Seahorse and dragonfly

Flat rounded stones are transformed with a painted image. Remember that the colours will darken when varnish is applied on top.

Fishing

The fish family

You can create many different types of fish, using a variety of different shaped pebbles. Use air-drying clay to join the pieces together and let your imagination do the rest!

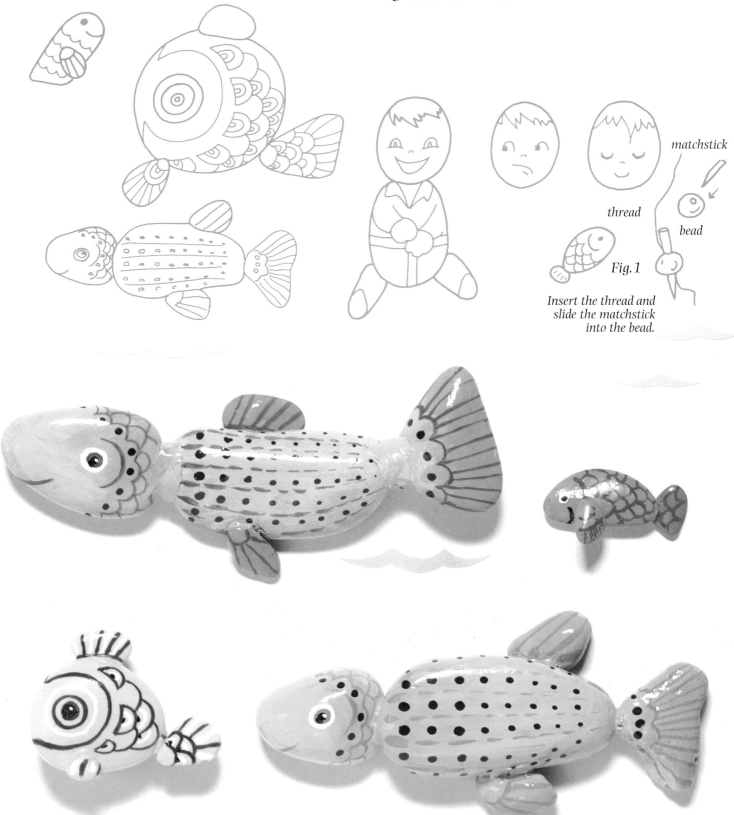

matchstick

thread

bead

Fig. 1

Insert the thread and slide the matchstick into the bead.

Fishermen

Create the three figures by gluing pebbles together. Paint each fishermen and add their different expressions. Use 12cm (5in) lengths of wire for their fishing-rods. Tie on ordinary thread for the line and thread a small bead through a matchstick to make the float (see Fig.1 opposite).

Faces and figures

Amusing likenesses can be painted on to round or oval pebbles. A smooth base of gouache is painted on first, then the cheeks are coloured with shades of pink. The features are then added, and finally any accessories. Here a gentleman's glasses are made out of thin wire and glued on to the pebble. The boy's hat is made out of a felt band which is attached to a felt peak. This fits neatly over the pebble.

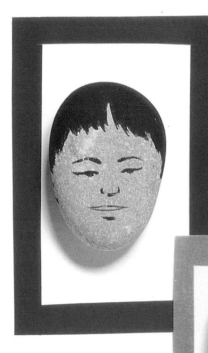

The natural colour of the stone can also be used to good effect; only the hair and features need be painted.

Fancy hats

Elegant hats can transform a pebble face into a fancy model which can be displayed on a small pedestal made from a length of dowel (Fig. 1) and a wooden base (Fig. 2). The hat is simply a felt ring which is positioned over the top of the pebble (Fig. 3). First, paint in the face. Try out various brims using thin paper before making the felt brim. Glue the brim to the pebble and paint the top of the pebble to match. You can embellish your hat with feathers, ribbons or paper flowers.

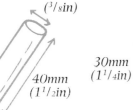

10mm
(³/₈in)

40mm
(1¹/₂in)

Fig. 1

30mm
(1¹/₄in)

30mm
(1¹/₄in)

Fig. 2

Fig. 3

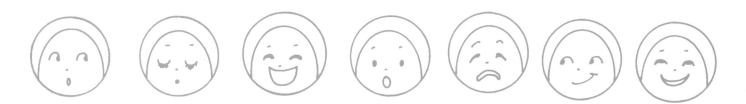

Babies

Two pebbles, joined with collars of air-drying clay, are used to make these cute babies. They are painted either pink or blue. The arms are modelled using air-drying clay. Notice how easy it is to change the expression and the character of each baby.

Triplets

Three small pebbles are glued to a smooth pebble base which is decorated with painted lace sheets and a blue floral cover.

Nanny

The nanny is painted on a triangular stone. The red scarf is knitted using fine needles and thin yarn. It is then carefully transferred on to two wooden cocktail sticks and glued into position.

Baby in a pram

The pram is painted on to an oval pebble; the head and wheels are then glued into position. The handle is made out of air-drying clay.

The circus

Large oval and long flat pebbles are used to create most of these circus characters. You may have to add small balancing pebbles to help them stand upright. The conical hats are made out of cones of paper and the ring-masters 'hat' is just a paper brim (see page 27). The juggling clown has two arms made out of card. He is juggling balls which are small beads glued on to thin wire; this is bent, then glued to each hand.

length of wire

beads

Juggling clown

Ringmaster

Performing seal

Chequered clown

White clown

Acrobatic dog

Cut this shape from thin card
and glue the flap to edge A to
make a conical hat.

A

Note
It is advisable to wedge any models which do not
have a flat base, so that they stay upright. Glue
small flat pebbles into gaps at the base to balance a
model.

Pebble pictures

Flowers and foliage

Flowers and leaves can be painted on to smooth pebbles. Textured backgrounds make a good contrast, or flat colour can be laid in to complement the design.

Buildings

Choose a pebble to complement the shape of your design. The image can be painted directly on to the surface, using the texture of the stone as a background. Add sky or foliage to create depth and interest.

Town house

Farm

Villa

Castle

Landscapes

Blues, greens and white are used to create these
small landscapes; they are painted on to pale
grey or cream pebbles.

Windy day

Snowy peaks

Stormy sea

Summer fields

35

Enchanted forest

Children will love this magical scene. Choose bright colours and use a fine brush for the abstract designs, features and details.

Mushrooms and elves

Choose long pebbles for the mushroom stems and flat, rounded pebbles for the caps. Add air-drying clay to the bases to give balance and glue the caps to the stems. Small, pointed pebbles are ideal for the elves' bodies and heads, which are joined with air-drying clay.

The three wise monkeys

The arms and legs are made out of air-drying clay. The heads and bodies are assembled and glued first, then the limbs are attached and moulded into position, and the monkeys are glued on to the stone base. They are then painted and varnished.

Zodiac

Twelve small pebbles and one larger one are needed for this model. The base is a 25cm (10in) circle of card covered with wrapping paper. The border pebbles are painted, varnished and glued into position. Finally, the radiating lines are drawn in, then the larger pebble is painted, varnished and secured in the centre of the design.

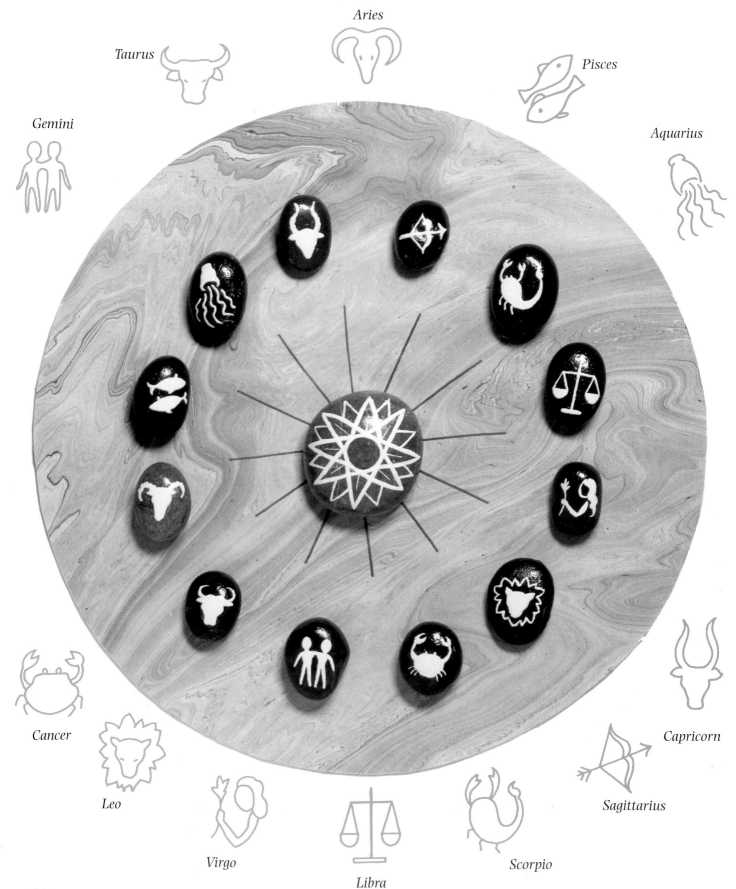

Aries

Taurus

Pisces

Gemini

Aquarius

Cancer

Capricorn

Leo

Sagittarius

Virgo

Scorpio

Libra

Trompe l'oeil

Trompe l'oeil means 'deceiving the eye'. Here, a sheet of gift wrap with a sky and cloud design has been used to good effect, although any design could be chosen. Draw the shape of the window on to tracing paper and transfer the image on to a selected area of the gift wrap. Carefully cut out the shape and glue it on to the pebble. Use paint to create the impression of torn paper round the edge of the window.

Leisure activities

Tennis

A round smooth pebble is ideal for this racket head. The handle and ball are made out of air-drying clay, which is moulded and attached when wet, then painted when dry.

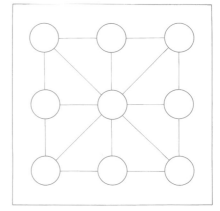

Rugby ball

This pebble is the ideal shape!

Board game

Any simple board game can be created using pebbles as counters or pieces. You will need the appropriate number of pebbles, all of them similar in shape and size. Here, the board base is covered with coloured paper, and the game is draw in using felt-tip pens. The pebbles are painted in contrasting colours.

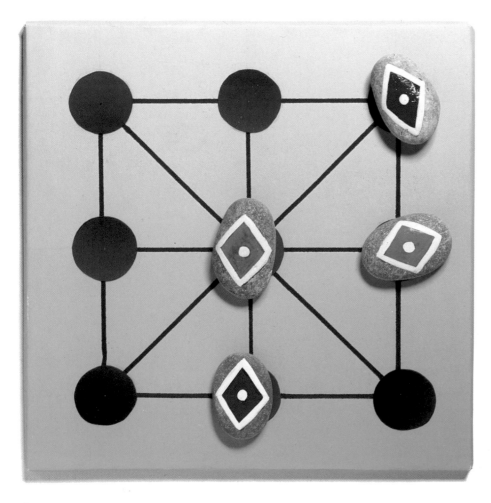

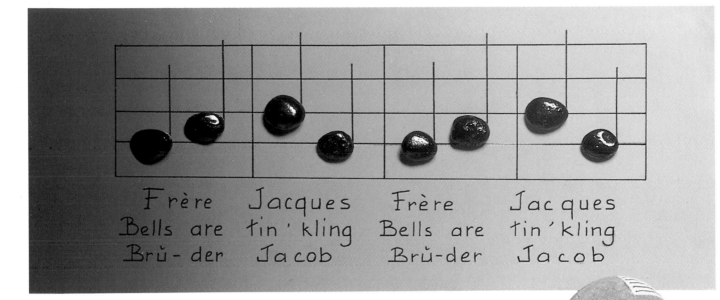

Frère   Jacques   Frère   Jacques
Bells are   tin'kling   Bells are   tin'kling
Brŭ-der   Jacob   Brŭ-der   Jacob

Music

Here are some amusing musical designs. The small, round notes are painted and varnished, then positioned on a score drawn on to coloured card with a fine felt-tip. The bigger, individual notes are traced, then painted on to plain pebbles. For the musical spiral, a band of white is painted on to a larger stone, then the score lines and notes are added with a fine felt-tip pen. A brightly painted keyboard completes the scene.

Dor - mez   - vous?   Dor - mez - vous ?
Work   be - gins   Work   be - gins
Schla - fen   Sie ?   Schla - fen · Sie ?

41

Christmas

Similarly shaped pebbles are used for the Christmas tree and Father Christmas. The base of the tree and Santa's sack are both painted pebbles which are glued into position. An elongated stone forms the background for the shooting star. This could also be painted on a pebble which has been coloured dark blue or black.

Snowflakes

Stencils could be used to create these lovely snowflake crystals, or the designs can be traced then transferred to the surface of the pebbles. The patterns are painted in using a fine brush and white gouache.

43

Tempting food

Fruit and vegetables

This appetising assortment uses a variety of shapes.
Gather together your pebbles and see how they can be
transformed into different types of food. Study fruit
and vegetables before you start to paint. The flat, base
colours should be painted in first, then tones, details
and highlights added afterwards.

44

Sausages and egg

Elongated pebbles are ideal for these sausage designs – the size does not matter; they could be small or large. A smooth, flat pebble is used for the fried egg, and this is painted white. The yolk is modelled from air-drying clay which is painted yellow when it has hardened and then glued on to the egg white.

Icecream

The icecream fits snugly on to a pebble that is tapered at one end. The texture of the cone is painted on and then paler colours are added to highlight areas of the design.

45

Weather vane

This weather vane is made from a large, heavy, pebble with a flat, steady base. Points of the compass are painted on to the surface. Two coats of varnish are then applied to make the design more durable. A 5cm (2in) length of plastic tube is inserted into a small ball of air-drying clay. This is then secured to the centre of the design, so that the tube stands vertically. The card wind sock is glued to a 10cm (4in) length of stiff wire, and this is then inserted in the tube. Make sure that the wind sock revolves freely so that it can indicate which way the wind is blowing.

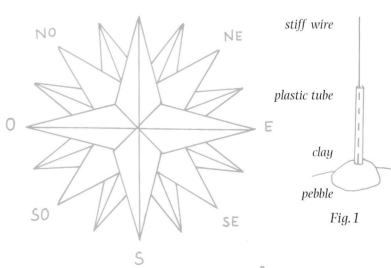

wind sock

stiff wire

plastic tube

clay

pebble

Fig. 1

Natural colours

Nature has decorated some of her pebbles far better than any artist could. If you are lucky enough to find beautifully shaped and patterned stones like these, wash them carefully. When dry, the veins on smooth pebbles may appear dull and indistinct; this can be rectified by highlighting them with white paint, then varnishing them. The varnish will enrich the natural colours of the stone and create a lovely glossy finish. Study textured pebbles carefully. They may not need much paint, but a small hollow or recess in the surface of the pebble, or some other irregularity may indicate an eye – or suggest another feature.

Index